"The old town, with its irregular houses, stage above stage hardly resembles the work of men, it is more like a piling up of rocks; and I cannot attempt to describe what we saw ... but must say that, high as my expectations had been raised, the city of Edinburgh surpassed all expectation."

Dorothy Wordsworth, Journal, 16th Sep. 1803

"Who indeed, that has once seen Edinburgh ... but must see it again in dreams waking or sleeping? My dear Sir, do not think I blaspheme when I tell you that your great London, as compared to Dun-Edin ... is as prose compared to poetry."

Charlotte Brontë, Letter to W. Smith Williamson, 1850

"... Edinburgh (in my estimation the most beautiful city in Britain)"

HRH The Prince of Wales, *A Vision of Britain*
Published by Doubleday 1989

Moubray House

MAXWELL J. WRIGHT

OLD EDINBURGH

A Walk
Through History

First published in 1997 by
Appin Publishers
21 Keston Gardens
Keston
Kent BR2 6BL

Copyright © 1997 Maxwell J. Wright

ISBN 0-9530680-0-5

A catalogue record for this book is available from
the British Library

Maxwell J. Wright's right to be identified as the author
of this work has been asserted by him in accordance with
the Copyright, Designs and Patents Act 1988.

Typeset in New Century 11/13pt by
Scriptmate Editions
Manufacture coordinated in UK by
Book-in-Hand Ltd 20 Shepherds Hill, London N6 5AH

Edinburgh is not only beautiful, it is also rich in history, particularly at the ancient heart of the city, set on its ridge between Castle and Palace. For those whose time is limited this is the story of the Old Town, followed by a detailed description of the author's favourite walk in the Royal Mile — A Walk Through History.

Acknowledgments

I am grateful to all other writers on Edinburgh subjects, for providing an unfailing source of pleasure and information over the years. For some points of detail I am particularly indebted to two modern works, *The Making of Classical Edinburgh* by A.J. Youngman (Edinburgh University Press 1966) and *Edinburgh, an Illustrated Architectural Guide* by Charles McKean (Royal Incorporation of Architects in Scotland/Scottish Academic Press 1982).

For her wise input and considerable patience I thank my wife Joan, and dedicate this book to her.

Contents

INTRODUCTION

"Where the huge Castle holds its state
And all the steep slope down,
Whose ridgy back heaves to the sky
Piled deep and massy, close and high,
Mine own Romantic Town."

Sir Walter Scott 1771–1832

All visitors inevitably find themselves in Princes Street, and from here the view across the valley has hardly changed from Scott's poetic description of nearly two hundred years ago. When Scott was born in 1772, Princes Street where you now stand was green pastureland, and Edinburgh was confined to the crest and sides of the ridge above you, still today covered with old buildings and crowned with spires and steeples.

Sir Walter Scott was a native of Edinburgh, a lover of Scottish history and a great romantic — most visitors with any sense of history or romance would also like to visit the Old Town, but hardly know how long it would take, where to begin and which direction to follow.

This little book sets out to fill this need — a single walk through the essential heart of Old Edinburgh, taking only an hour or two or as long as you wish. The great National Monuments such as The Castle, St Giles and Holyrood Palace should of course be visited but are not part of this itinerary, which is my own favourite saunter through the old city.

Although the description of the walk stands by itself, it is essentially a journey through the past, and the book therefore includes short sections on Scottish history as it relates to Edinburgh, on the architecture and development of the city, and on the historical characters who walked these streets. It would greatly add to your enjoyment if you can browse through these notes before setting out, or turn to the pages indicated during your short expedition.

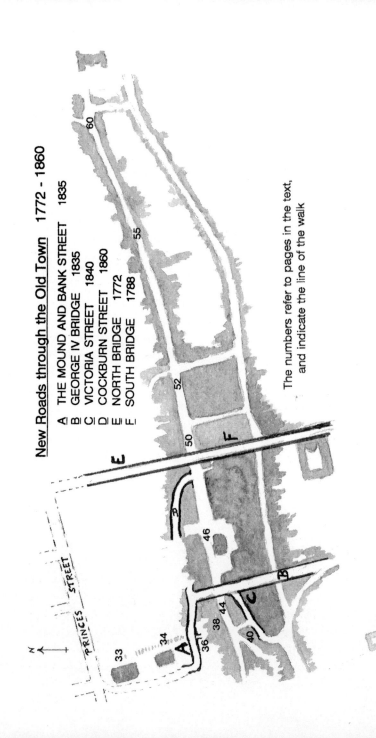

New Roads through the Old Town 1772 - 1860

- **A** THE MOUND AND BANK STREET 1835
- **B** GEORGE IV BRIDGE 1835
- **C** VICTORIA STREET 1840
- **D** COCKBURN STREET 1860
- **E** NORTH BRIDGE 1772
- **F** SOUTH BRIDGE 1788

The numbers refer to pages in the text,
and indicate the line of the walk

THE OLD TOWN

Europe is rich in ancient cities. Many of these have a medieval core which is still there to be explored, although in others such as London this core has largely vanished under the pressures of modern development. Its survival in other cities is often an accident of geography, a central area spared because subsequent development has occurred around it rather than within it. It may be a riverside site where the other side of the river has proved more attractive for modern needs, or an old seaport which has silted up and then been sited elsewhere. Sometimes the original town was built on a hill or a ridge, which then proved too steep and less accessible for modern living or commercial purposes.

Old Edinburgh is built on such a ridge, sloping down from The Castle high on its rock to the Palace of Holyrood at the bottom, and owes its survival to this physical separation from the New Town which developed across the valley in the late 18th century. This new development lay roughly parallel to the old, and only two major roads with ingenious connecting bridges crossed the Old Town at right angles, causing some local destruction at those points but preserving the line of the old street.

The Castle rock is the oldest part of the city. Accessible at only one point and almost impregnable, it is now known to have been inhabited from prehistoric times. It contains the oldest surviving building in Edinburgh, the charming 12th-Century Saint Margaret's Chapel, and when this was built the town was already clustering in the Castle's shadow at the top of the ridge. At the very bottom of the ridge a mile away a magnificent Abbey and then a Royal Palace arose, and by early medieval times the town had spread down from Castle to Abbey, the line of the street being preserved to this day and still referred to as The Royal Mile.

To the south lay another valley and in this a second parallel street developed called the Cowgate. A steep and winding hill, the West Bow, connected the two streets at the upper end, with two further connecting streets at a lower level. Scores of narrow passages called 'closes' descended on each side of the ridge, to the Cowgate on the south and to a stretch of water on the north called the Nor' Loch, where Princes Street Gardens now lie.

The basic anatomy of the old city was thus quite simple but the system of closes was very complicated, a medieval warren of buildings of all shapes and heights, housing both rich and poor. The finest houses usually fronted on to the Royal Mile or the Cowgate, and in 1530 a European visitor wrote of these streets "Nothing here is humble or lowly but everything magnificent."

In the two centuries to 1560 the population grew from about 10,000 to about 30,000, but the area of the city did not, due primarily to the confining effect of the City Walls …

THE CITY WALLS

The city was protected to the west and north by the Castle rock and the Nor' Loch, but due to the ever-present threat from England a City Wall was built in 1450 to complete the protective ring. This was later enlarged to include the Cowgate, but the area enclosed was still relatively small for the expanding population. The townspeople were reluctant to build outside the protection of the walls, and the only solution was to build higher and yet higher, with many of the closes becoming narrow ravines where sunlight hardly penetrated. The situation of the town on a ridge further compounded the situation, since even buildings of moderate height at the street front could be many storeys high at the back. The City Chambers illustrates this — a modest four storeys fronting the High Street is eleven storeys in height when viewed from Princes Street; and other buildings rose as high as fourteen storeys. After 1745 the Walls, along with their fine gateways (known as 'ports') were gradually demolished, but several stretches of Wall survive along with many of the tall buildings which are a legacy of the old walled city.

THE LANDS

These tall tenement buildings, mostly dating from the 16th to the 18th-Centuries are known as 'lands', and they largely determined the past social life of Edinburgh. While in England the upper classes of the 18th century had already moved to handsome Georgian streets and squares, this did not occur in Edinburgh until much later in that century. Certainly there were some fine mansions and courtyards, but the bulk of the people both rich and poor lived in these tall lands, and Peer and commoner, tradesman and servant, all passed each other on the ubiquitous spiral staircase and knew each other's business.

Your status determined the height at which you lived — the cellar was a storeroom, and the ground floor usually a shop or workshop. Above that lived the tradesmen and the poorer families, and above that the merchants and professional classes. The apartments near the top of the building were high above the smells and noise of the street, and here dwelt the nobleman and his household, with his servants sleeping in the garret or on the stairway. This arrangement made for a robust social life embracing all classes of society. Entertainment was provided by innumerable taverns and brothels, while Assembly Rooms, strictly supervised as regards social etiquette, catered for balls and other more formal occasions. As described later on page 46, the Market Cross outside St Giles was the focus of outdoor social and commercial life.

OLD TOWN ARCHITECTURE

To the present-day first-time visitor, the tall stone buildings of the Old Town may come as something of a surprise. This is particularly true of Southern English visitors, who are more accustomed to delightful old towns consisting largely of picturesque timber-framed buildings which are rarely more than four storeys in height. Continental visitors are less surprised, because tall stone buildings are often a feature of the old quarters of European cities.

For those who like to pick out architectural features, the following building types can be identified:

(1) *Thick-Walled Stone Buildings,* in the form of:

   a) Small irregular stones, known as Harled Rubble, often with larger stones around the window frames. This is the commonest building material, and is a sure sign of an old house. The stone becomes very dark over the centuries, but can be cleaned back to its original pleasant whitish-yellow hue.

   b) Polished Ashlar — cut blocks of stone a foot or more in height laid in courses. This is a very handsome and expensive building material, used for the more prestigious buildings. The front of Gladstone's Land in the Lawnmarket and the Canongate Tolbooth are good examples. The flatter cut stone of a later period is less attractive.

   c) Red Sandstone from Dumfriesshire — this is included for completeness, as it is often seen in the Royal Mile, usually indicating 19th-Century rebuilding or infilling. The horrendously ugly building materials of the 1960s and 1970s are (with one exception at the foot of Brodie's Close) mercifully absent from the Royal Mile!

(2) *Timber-Framed Buildings*. Some structural timber-framing of the upper storeys of stone buildings did occur in the 16th century. There are only a very few of these left, such as Huntly House in the Canongate, recognisable by the slight overhang of the upper storeys.

(3) *Timber Galleries*. Drawings and old photographs of the Royal Mile and its closes show what appears to be an attractive profusion of timbered buildings. In fact most of these were enclosed timbered-gallery additions to the stone buildings. Today almost all of this outside woodwork has been removed or has rotted away, but a drawing of 1879 shows Regent Morton's House in Blackfriar's Street resplendent with overhanging wooden balconies, quite different from its present appearance. The Earl of Hertford in the brief English invasion of 1544 sacked the Canongate (which lay outside the City Wall) and left it burning to his satisfaction, but in fact it was the timber galleries which were burning, and the stone structures behind were largely undamaged. John Knox's House is about the only remaining example of a galleried house.

HISTORY AND PERSONALITIES OF OLD EDINBURGH

The history of Edinburgh is bound up with that of Scotland, whose Capital City it has been for centuries. For a clearer understanding the history is here divided into three periods ...Pre-1561; 1561 to 1745; and Post-1745.

Pre-1561

This is the era in which Edinburgh expanded from a small settlement crouching under the protection of the Castle Rock to a bustling medieval city. Initially it consisted of low timbered or stone buildings, with long narrow gardens running down either side of the ridge and divided from each other by narrow lanes. However by 1561 the great stone lands were beginning to rise, forced ever higher by the expanding population; the gardens were soon built over, and the lanes between them became the narrow Closes.

In early medieval times Scotland was a civilised and relatively tranquil country, and had acquired an early sense of national identity unusual in Europe at that time — it has been said that Scotland had all the advantages of Norman culture without the disadvantages of Norman conquest. This scene altered in the late 13th century, when Scotland began her long struggle to keep her national independence against the expansionist policies of her powerful neighbour, England.

Throughout this period Scotland was allied to France, and it was from France in 1561 that Mary Queen of Scots came as an eighteen-year-old girl to begin her reign as the rightful heir of the Royal House of Stuart.

1561–1745

Any understanding of Scotland's and Edinburgh's history depends on a consideration of this middle period. It begins with Mary Stuart's accession to the throne and ends with the departure from the city of her great-great-great-grandson Prince Charles Edward Stuart nearly two hundred years later.

Most of the features of interest that we shall pass date from this period, and a visitor from those years would find much to recognise in the present-day Royal Mile.

Century	Opposing Parties	Personalities
16th	Catholic v Protestant	Mary Queen of Scots John Knox Regent Morton King James VI
17th	Royalist v Covenanter	Marquis of Montrose Marquis of Argyll Oliver Cromwell Viscount Dundee
18th	Jacobite v Hanoverian	Prince Charles Edward Stuart Duke of Cumberland

This little chart is a simplification, in some respects an oversimplification, but provides a basic framework for an understanding of the tangled politics of the period. For example, a Catholic family of the 16th century would tend to be Royalist in the 17th century (although perhaps no longer Catholic) and Jacobite in the early 18th century; and likewise their opposite numbers.

There were certainly exceptions to this, where a family could be divided in its loyalties, or where an individual felt constrained to place one loyalty above another — for example, the Marquis of Montrose (see page 25).

The first rift came with the Reformation, when Mary Queen of Scots, newly widowed and devoutly Catholic, returned to a country which was now overwhelmingly Protestant under the leadership of John Knox. She made no attempt to reverse Protestantism, but her own Catholic practices infuriated Knox.

John Knox and The Reformation

The Reformation, which swept Europe in the 16th century, stemmed from different causes in different countries, but in general arose from the growing nationalist spirit of Western Europe fretting under the domination of Rome. In some countries the movement was fanned by the excessive wealth and corruption of the senior Catholic clergy, and nowhere was this more true than in Scotland. Attempts at reform were rigorously resisted by the Catholic Church and several burnings of heretics took place. One of these early martyrs was George Wishart, who was always accompanied by a black-bearded cleric named John Knox. Knox escaped Wishart's fate, but was subsequently captured by the French and sent to the galleys. Freed at the intercession of the young Protestant king, Edward VI of England, he continued to serve the Protestant cause in England, Germany and Switzerland, and eventually returned to Scotland for good in 1559.

Despite his forbidding image, Knox was an astute and far-sighted politician who worked for stronger ties with England as opposed to the old alliance with Catholic France. This inevitably brought him into contention with the newly crowned Mary Queen of Scots, but by the time Knox died in 1572 Mary had abdicated, the Presbyterian Church was firmly established, and the stage was set for Union of the Scottish and English crowns thirty years later.

The ancient house in the High Street, where he is believed to have lived, is strongly evocative of the period and of his role in it.

Mary Queen of Scots (1542–1587)

Mary became queen when only one week old. Sent to France at the age of six, she married the Dauphin, and was briefly Queen of France until her husband died in 1560. Returning as a young widow at the age of eighteen to assume her Scottish throne, she determined not to impose her own strong Catholic faith on her Presbyterian subjects, and deliberately surrounded herself with Protestant courtiers and advisers.

This however did not save her from the wrath of Knox, who objected to her Catholic practices and indeed disliked the whole idea of women in authority. Mary's life in Holyrood Palace was made wretched not only by Knox's continual sermonising, but also by a horrific incident in which her Secretary and confidant, David Rizzio, was brutally murdered in her presence by her jealous husband, Lord Darnley, and his friends. This unwise marriage to the worthless young Darnley ended eventually in his own assassination, an event in which the Earl of Bothwell, a charming but reckless Protestant, was heavily involved. Whether or not Mary had prior knowledge of the murder, her subsequent marriage to Bothwell only eight weeks later was a further gross error of judgement which finally alienated many Catholics and Protestants alike. Supporters rallied to her cause but were defeated in successive battles, and Mary was forced to abdicate in 1567 in favour of her infant son, James VI, and fled to England. Hoping for sanctuary there, she was instead imprisoned for many years, and at the age of forty-five was executed by her cousin, Queen Elizabeth.

Mary has sometimes been harshly judged by history. She was very young, only twenty-four years old when forced to abdicate, and had a passionate nature which led to fatal errors of judgement. But she attempted tolerant rule in an intolerant and explosive age, and given her circumstances was probably in an impossible position from the start. By birth she was the most highly-placed figure of her age — Dowager Queen

Tower and Crown of St Giles. In 1571 a detachment of troops loyal to the defeated Queen Mary held out in the Tower for five months

of France, Queen of Scotland, and with a legitimate claim to the throne of England; a recipe for success in the eyes of history or of tragedy, which latter proved to be the case.

What remains is a figure of beauty, warm affection, and ability, who charmed all but the most bigoted, and above all of courage and steadfast adherence to her faith.

In Edinburgh she lived in her chambers at Holyrood Palace and in The Castle, but the Royal Mile witnessed many a Royal Progress, beginning with the lavish procession of welcome when she arrived to claim her throne in 1561. Her last and saddest procession took place six years later after her defeat at the battle of Carberry Hill, when she was led up the Royal Mile amid the derision of the mob, to lodge briefly in a house near Advocate's Close on her way to exile and imprisonment.

Regent Morton (died 1581)

James Douglas, Earl of Morton, joined the Reformers early in his career, and was one of the Protestant nobles who fought against Mary and secured her downfall. A powerful figure of his day, he became Regent of Scotland in 1572 during the minority of King James VI. Nine years later he was toppled by a political coup, charged with being implicated in the murder of Darnley, and beheaded.

His town mansion in Blackfriars Street still exists today.

Bishop Adam Bothwell

Adam Bothwell, Bishop of Orkney, performed the controversial Protestant Wedding Ceremony between Mary Queen of Scots and his (unrelated) namesake the Earl of Bothwell in the Chapel Royal at Holyrood in 1567. Censured for this by his colleagues, he was obliged subsequently to preach a sermon acknowledging his guilt; but his character surmounted this setback, and he retained his high office in the Reformed Church and eventually died in his own house, which still exists and is visible from Advocate's Close. Incidentally his nephew John Napier (1560–1617) also has his place in history as the inventor of logarithms.

Bailie John McMorran (died 1595)

A period of comparative political quiet settled upon Edinburgh after the turmoil of Queen Mary's reign. However the Nobility and the increasingly influential Town Council were frequently at loggerheads, and furthermore — like most European cities — the streets could be violent and riots were commonplace.

In September 1595 one such riot took place at the recently built High School, where the boys — mostly the sons of gentlemen or noblemen — having been refused a request for a week's holiday, had obtained weapons and barricaded themselves into the building. Bailie McMorran, a wealthy and influential merchant and town councillor, was sent to treat with the miscreants but, receiving only shouted threats and missiles, ordered the door to be battered down. While this was being done a single shot rang out, and the good Bailie dropped dead with a pistol ball through his head. The terrified boys then surrendered and were quick to offer up the culprit, one William Sinclair, a boy of noble family.

A battle of wills then took place between Nobility and Town Council on the fate of the boy and the question of reparation; the King himself was invoked, and somewhat reluctantly and on the grounds of expediency came down on the side of the nobles, so the Council — and the McMorran family — had to be satisfied with an apology from Lord Sinclair's family and a short term of banishment for the miscreant.

Bailie John's fine house, still standing behind the Lawnmarket, passed to his brother Ninian McMorran; and three years after the sad event the little courtyard was again ablaze with light and colour as the Town Council, having made its peace with King James, hosted a fine banquet for the King and his court in this very house.

Bailie Macmorran's House

The National Covenant and The Marquis of Montrose (1612–1650)

King James VI left Edinburgh for London in 1603 on acceding to the throne of the newly formed United Kingdom. He promised to return every three years, but in fact returned only once in 1617. His son Charles I visited again in 1633, and a primary purpose of both visits was to impose the same kind of Episcopalian church government and form of worship that prevailed in England. To counter this, a lengthy document named The National Covenant was compiled by distinguished Scottish lawyers, and on 28th February 1638 was signed by great numbers of people on a flat tombstone in Greyfriars Churchyard. This professed continued loyalty to the King, but repudiated the new English Prayer Book and demanded the removal of bishops.

As the Civil War flared in England, the Scottish Army supported whichever side appeared to favour The Covenant, which was first the Parliament and then the King. As a result of this, Oliver Cromwell twice entered Edinburgh, first as an ally and honoured guest in 1648, and then as a victorious general in 1650 after the execution of Charles I.

During this period of bitterness and division in Scotland one honourable name stands out above all others, that of the Marquis of Montrose, the "Great Marquis" of Scottish legend. He was a man of learning and great courage, and a soldier of genius. Although a Covenanter, he judged his loyalty to his king to lie above all other considerations, and did splendid service for the royal cause in Scotland. He therefore became hated and reviled by the Covenanters, and after many victories he was eventually defeated in battle and betrayed to his enemies. Taken to Edinburgh, and carried in a cart up the Canongate through a mob whipped up by the Covenanting ministers, he faced his enemy the Marquis of Argyll beneath the balcony of Moray House (as described on page 56), and passed to his death with his dignity and courage unimpaired.

Ten years later, after the Restoration, his remains were gathered and buried with great ceremony in St Giles Cathedral, and a fine memorial raised over them.

The Marquis of Argyll (1598–1661)

Archibald Campbell, 1st Marquis of Argyll, was Montrose's political enemy and a committed Covenanter. In Moray House in 1648 he held discussions with Oliver Cromwell at which the question of King Charles I's fate was discussed, although Argyll himself was uneasy with the proposal that the King be executed. When the execution took place in London in 1649, Argyll along with all sections of Scottish opinion was deeply shocked that Scotland, through English action, was now without a King, and Argyll made contact with his heir Prince Charles, and had him proclaimed King

Charles II in Edinburgh. Despite this, on the Restoration of Charles II in 1660, Argyll's political enemies made sure that he was arrested as a regicide. As he lay in Edinburgh Castle awaiting execution he could hear the fanfare of trumpets and firing of guns in the city celebrating the rehabilitation and ceremonial re-burial of Montrose in St Giles.

Argyll died nobly and rather less cruelly than Montrose, his head being affixed to the same spike on the Tolbooth from which Montrose's head had only lately been removed. In due course he too got a fine memorial in St Giles, and there in the gloom still lie the two great adversaries separated only by the width of the nave. His impressive town mansion, Moray House, still dominates the Canongate.

Sir William Dick (died 1655)

Sir William was Lord Provost of Edinburgh at the time of the Civil War, and one of the merchant princes of Scotland. He was said to have ships on every sea and to be worth over £200,000 — a huge fortune in those days — and one could imagine nothing going wrong with such a successful life.

Unfortunately for him, his great wealth inevitably involved him in politics. Although not at heart a Royalist, he had a great personal dislike for Oliver Cromwell, so after much indecision he sent £20,000 to support Charles I and his Royalist army. This was swallowed up like a drop in the ocean, and he contributed again and yet again. When Cromwell finally marched into Edinburgh and fined him a further £65,000 he was unable to raise the money, and Sir William was sent to London where he died in bitter poverty in the common prison in 1655.

He lived in the house which you can view from Advocate's Close, which had been owned by Bishop Adam Bothwell in the previous century (see page 48).

Viscount Dundee, John Graham of Claverhouse (1649–1689)

Charles II ("whose word no man relies on") despite having signed the Covenant in 1649 in order to secure his own position, had no intention at his Restoration of carrying out its obligations. He packed the Scottish Parliament with reliable Royalists, re-introduced bishops, and appointed Claverhouse, a ruthless professional soldier, to suppress the Covenanters. This he did with great cruelty, still evoked by many a mossy tombstone in the remote moors and glens of Scotland where his dragoons operated.

Many a sad procession took place to the foot of the West Bow, where the brave but stubborn Covenanters "glorified God in the Grassmarket", and from the old houses still overlooking it Claverhouse would sometimes watch the proceedings.

'The Killing Times' ended with the expulsion of King James VII (James II of England) in 1688, and the following year Claverhouse was killed in his moment of victory, supporting the deposed King at the Battle of Killiecrankie.

Despite his tainted record, he was in some respects a gallant and romantic figure, viewed either as "Bonnie Dundee" or "Bloody Claverhouse" depending on one's political and religious persuasion.

The Union of The Parliaments (1707) and *Bonnie Prince Charlie* (1720–1788)

Following the Glorious Revolution of 1688 Scotland returned to a period of relative tranquillity, although relations with England remained severely strained.

In 1707 the Commissioners of Scotland and England had agreed an Act of Union of The Parliaments, and met in Edinburgh for the Signing. The mob, fearful of the consequences for Scottish independence and suspicious (with some cause) that some of the Commissioners were acting to their own financial advantage, ran riot in the streets and prevented the Signing in The Parliament Hall. The Commissioners, by now thoroughly alarmed, took refuge in a summerhouse (see page 55) in the grounds of Moray House, but then had to flee again to an underground cellar near the Tron Church. There the Signing was finally completed, and the messenger bearing the document escaped by night on the road to London.

On March 25th The Scottish Parliament met for the last time under the beautiful hammer-beam roof of Parliament Hall. "We are bought and sold for English gold," declared the Jacobites, and while Edinburgh settled down and tried to reap the advantages of the new Union, the Jacobites bided their time.

After an abortive rising in 1715, their time came in 1745. The story of Prince Charles Edward Stuart's attempt to restore the Stuart dynasty is well known — his landing in Scotland and victorious progress to Derby, within 120 miles of London and a good chance of victory; then, due to pressure from his commanders and against his own instincts, the return to Scotland, defeat at Culloden Moor, dramatic escape to France, and forty years of frustration and exile.

During his progress south the Prince's Highland Army captured Edinburgh, which he entered through the Netherbow Port on September 17th, 1745. He stayed for six weeks, issuing from the city only once to defeat General Cope's army at Prestonpans. Many in the city welcomed him, for despite some weaknesses in his character he was educated, charming, brave and chivalrous — a complete contrast to the reigning sovereign George II, a remote Germanic figure who had never been anywhere near Scotland; and an even greater contrast to his son, the boorish, cruel, and sadistic Duke of Cumberland ('Butcher Cumberland').

After taking Edinburgh, the Prince's father was proclaimed King James III at the Market Cross, and Holyrood became again a truly Royal Palace, hosting receptions and balls which provided a lifetime's cherished memories for the young ladies of the Capital.

However all was not entirely well with the Prince's cause in Edinburgh. Elements of the Hanoverian army had retreated to the Castle, and isolated exchanges of fire and roving patrols from both sides made the upper end of The Royal Mile and the West Bow unsafe. Furthermore the Establishment and the business community remained passively opposed to the Prince; they had moved all notes and money to the Castle, and refused to resume normal commercial business during the Occupation. Much of the Prince's time and energy was therefore devoted to raising money and equipment on a day-to-day basis as best he could, to the detriment of normal city government. However several Lowland gentlemen rallied to his cause with their retainers, and his army now comprised some five thousand men with limited cavalry, being no longer the purely Highland army with which he had begun his campaign.

On November 1st, 1745 the Prince and his army left Edinburgh, never to return. After Culloden the Jacobite cause never revived, and lived on only in memory and folklore.

The restoration of The Stuarts could have worked well — we shall never know — but the verdict of history is that the cause was already an anachronism in the hard-headed business-orientated 18th century, and Edinburgh, despite much strong sentiment to the contrary, appeared to have grasped this.

The Highlands suffered grievously under Butcher Cumberland's reprisals, but Edinburgh escaped the worst. Cumberland took pleasure in sleeping in the Prince's bed in Holyrood Palace, his Hessian mercenaries strutted briefly in The Royal Mile, and money and equipment to the value of £15,000 'borrowed' by the Prince was of course lost for ever.

The Lord Provost was put on trial in London but acquitted of active collaboration, and by the time the Prince died in Rome in 1788 Edinburgh itself had vastly changed.

1745 to Today

With the departure of the Prince, two hundred years of troubled history which began with the arrival of his great-great-great-grandmother Mary Queen of Scots in Edinburgh in 1561 effectively ended. The end of the '45 was almost like the lifting of a curse from the city — energies were diverted from the bitter politics of the last two centuries to more practical matters, and economically the city took off.

In 1752, only seven years after the '45, discussions began in the Council Chambers about expanding the city in such a way as to relieve the finally intolerable pressure building up within the walled confines of the medieval city. The key to this expansion, apart from the actual dismantling of walls and gates, was the building of a bridge over the deep valley to the North, and despite some local resistance and a fatal accident during construction, the North Bridge was built, and in 1772 was complete and open for traffic.

With the way open for the building of the elegant New Town, the aristocracy and then the middle classes began to move from the Old City. In a year or two the trickle grew to a flood, and by the turn of the century the streets and squares, largely planned by a young architect named James Craig, could rival anything London had to offer.

The New Town rapidly advanced down the hill towards the sea, and at the same time the city achieved an intellectual and literary height, a sort of talent boom which has seldom been surpassed in this country. This, along with its widely admired architecture, made it very much the in-place to visit, particularly as the prolonged Napoleonic Wars made European travel difficult.

There was however a social price to be paid. By the 1830s

the last of the moneyed classes had abandoned the closes and courtyards for more gracious living in the New Town. No longer did peer and commoner greet each other on the staircase, and only the poor remained in the Old Town. The tenements became grossly overcrowded, one being recorded as housing 248 people, without running water or toilet facilities. Occasionally an ancient land would collapse through neglect, one such incident killing 35 inhabitants.

London and other cities of course had a similar problem, but in the late 19th century there came an increasing social awareness and a large number of ancient buildings (probably about two-thirds) were swept away in Victorian improvements. Many of the narrow closes were opened out into courtyards, with only the most notable buildings surviving.

As the city became increasingly prosperous in a commercial and business sense, new roads were built involving the destruction of more closes — of an original three-hundred closes only about one hundred now remained. Two bridges now spanned the Cowgate to the South, still containing at that time its magnificent medieval mansions but by now a teeming slum. These bridges were and still are heavily disguised, being lined with houses rather like Old London Bridge, but with gaps over the Cowgate itself where well-to-do Victorians could stop their carriages and peer over at the lower orders swarming beneath. Fortunately the line of the Royal Mile and much of its building survived the Victorian improvements.

In the present century there has been a great revival of interest in the Old Town, coupled with the recognition that in itself it comprises a vast archaeological site. For instance, in 1940 an attempt to build underground bomb shelters in Mylne's Court, starting from an already deep wine cellar, revealed another four storeys of cellars before reaching bedrock. Similarly when the Tron Kirk ceased to be a church a few years ago, excavation under the floor revealed a Lost Close, complete

When the Tron Kirk was built in 1637, an ancient close called Marlin's Wynd was buried under the foundations, complete with cellars and drains and the cobbled street surface. The Tron Kirk was closed for worship in 1952, and Marlin's Wynd, long regarded as one of the 'lost closes' of Edinburgh, has now been partially uncovered and is open for viewing inside the church

with medieval cobbled surface, foundations and cellars, buried when the Church was built in 1637. In the Cowgate, close to the 17th-Century Tailor's Hall, 15th-Century buildings have recently been discovered, this time just beneath the ground; and during the building of the Scandic Crown Hotel another section of City Wall has come to light. The Old Town Renewal Trust, working from an ancient building in Advocates Close, is dedicated to investigating and preserving such finds.

Up to the 1930s large areas of the Old Town still looked much as they had for the past hundred years, the population much reduced and many still living in poverty in run-down historic buildings. The last few decades have seen a vast improvement in this situation, although inevitably in the process some more of Old Edinburgh has vanished and some has perhaps been 'over-prettified'. However, much remains, and what we now have is housing for the healthily increasing local population, both in the ancient buildings and in carefully structured modern developments — plus a pleasing blend of museums, student dwellings and small shops. It is to be hoped that future generations will continue to honour their historic responsibility toward the Old Town.

THE WALK

The Old Town is set on a sloping ridge, and our walk is essentially a gentle downhill stroll preceded by a short climb up the Playfair Steps to our high point. The climb is a pleasure in itself, since it affords fine views of both the Old and the New Town.

Start at the Royal Scottish Academy roughly at the centre of Princes Street, facing up towards the Old Town with the Royal Academy on your right. This building was the creation of the architect William Playfair in 1822–6, a Greek Doric-style temple later enlarged and rather incongruously topped by sphinxes and a statue of the young Queen Victoria seated surveying the New Town.

William Playfair was a fine architect, the 19th century successor to Craig, Adam and Chambers who so successfully designed the 18th-Century streets and squares of the New Town,

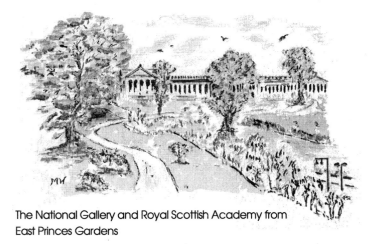

The National Gallery and Royal Scottish Academy from East Princes Gardens

and his work dominates this central area of Edinburgh linking the Old and the New Towns.

Next on your right is Playfair's National Gallery of 1845, much admired for its dignity and pleasing proportions. Playfair too was responsible for New College, the twin-towered building rearing above you, which represented a departure from his previous Classical style into the Gothic. The towers were designed in conjunction with the large spire of Tolbooth St John's Church behind to form a handsome architectural vista when viewed from Princes Street — handsome it is in its rather heavy Victorian style, but a great mass of ancient buildings was lost in the making of it, including the fine medieval palace of Mary of Guise, mother of Mary Queen of Scots.

Climb the steps, and half way up pause and look behind and around at the panorama of the New Town and Gardens, the general appearance of which has altered little since the pattern was finally set in the 1850s. The gardens in the valley, of which you are seeing only the eastern portion, are on the site of a loch which for centuries blocked access to what is now the New Town until drainage began in 1759 and the North Bridge was opened in 1772, succeeded in time by the present bridge which you can see spanning Waverley Station.

Drainage of the loch was completed in 1817 and the gardens were laid out between 1822 and 1849. At first they were private to the residents of Princes Street, but later keys were given out at an annual fee of £3 and eventually the gardens were fully opened to the public. In the Railway Boom of the 1840s stations had opened at both ends of Princes Street, but there was great resistance to the passage of the railway through the gardens. However by 1846 commercial pressure had won the day, and in that year the first train ran through the gardens, passing under the National Gallery and skirting the base of the Castle rock — Playfair was again called in to construct the embankment and stone walls screening the track.

The New Town from the Mound in 1829 (after the engraving by Thomas Shepherd). The Princes Street houses are lower than today, and more or less regular in height. The Royal Institution (now the Royal Scottish Academy) is in position, but as yet no National Gallery

Looking back at Princes Street and the New Town one admires the forethought of the City Fathers who decreed in 1817 that no commercial building would be permitted along its garden aspect, thus ensuring unencumbered views of the Castle and the Old Town from Princes Street. The Scott Monument is a dominant feature, an extravagant gothic fantasy of pinnacles and statuary completed in 1846 and quite out of keeping with classical Edinburgh — but it is great fun, and its fame is now such that without it Princes Street would be unrecognisable!

The Princes Street frontages are now a composite of styles and height, not entirely unattractive but certainly not as first built. A few of the original 18th-Century frontages are still visible dwarfed by their later neighbours. It is worth noting that, unlike other Georgian cities such as Bath, it was never intended that the 18th-Century New Town of Edinburgh should have uniform frontages, but there was a three-storey height restriction and this combination produced interest and variety while retaining cohesion.

Facing up again to the Old Town and looking right, the roadway up which the traffic labours is The Mound (originally called The Earthen Mound), ingeniously constructed around 1835 from the excavated soil dumped here as the New Town arose, and intended as a second link between the Old and New Towns — the North Bridge and The Mound have remained the only two major roadways crossing the Old Town, an important factor in keeping the Royal Mile more or less unspoiled by modern development (see illustration, page 10).

Beyond and above The Mound lies Ramsay Gardens, an attractive complex of buildings arranged around a quaint octagonal house built by the poet Allan Ramsay in the early 18th century, which you may be able to pick out with its curious irregular windows looking out over Princes Street.

At the top of the steps the tall tenements facing you on the left mainly date from the 17th and early 18th centuries. Cross the upper stretch of The Mound at the lights, and bear right and then forward (with the New College towers directly on your right), up a few more steps and under an archway into the Old Town, emerging into **Mylne's Court**. Robert Mylne was King's Master Mason, a respected architect who in 1690 conceived this courtyard as an early essay in town planning, demolishing several crowded closes to create this more open space. It remained a fashionable dwelling-place for over a century, one of the last places to retain upper-class residents after the exodus to the New Town. Immediately on your left is a moulded stone doorway at the foot of a spiral staircase — these moulded doorways are a feature of the Old Town, often surmounted by dates or pious texts, and you will see many of them as you walk.

Go forward again through another ancient passageway, and you will emerge into daylight in the upper part of the Royal Mile, this stretch being known as the **Lawnmarket**, where cloth ('lawn') was sold at open stalls in the street. We shall shortly look at it more closely, but first enter the next close on your left and bear right so as to wander through **James' Court**

... into the Old Town

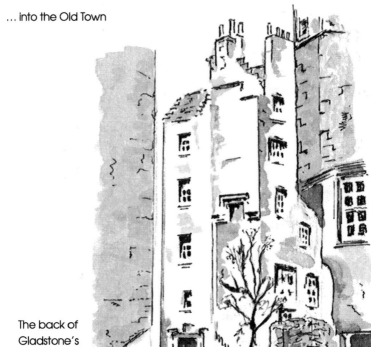

The back of
Gladstone's
Land

and **Wardrop Court**, keeping roughly parallel to the Royal Mile. These quaint courtyards were fashioned out of more crowded closes, and many of the buildings are 17th or 18th century or earlier. On your left is **Lady Stair's House**, dating from 1622; it was purchased and thus saved from demolition by Lord Roseberry, who however so over-restored it as to be barely recognisable from the outside as the ancient building it is. Originally it was confined in a long narrow close — hence its narrow shape which looks a little uncomfortable in its present exposed position — and had a terraced garden descending to the Nor' loch. The building had a romantic history which Sir Walter incorporated in his short story, *My Aunt Margaret's Mirror*. It is now the Burns, Scott and Stevenson Museum, and among other internal features has a stone stair with steps of irregular height to trip intruders!

On your right are the backs of the old houses of the Lawnmarket, including the older (16th century) portion of Gladstone's Land — which we shall see again from the front. Follow the courtyards round as far as you can, then emerge again into the Lawnmarket and admire the handsome facade of **Gladstone's Land**. This was erected by Thomas Gladstone, a prosperous merchant and ancestor of Prime Minister Gladstone, in 1617–20, grafted on to the earlier 16th-Century house. It shows all the best features of old Edinburgh buildings — finely crafted ashlar stone, an outside staircase (forestair), small pointed gables, and even the ground-floor arcading once common in the city. Internally it is of great interest, with fine rooms and painted walls and rafters dating from the 16th century. It is in the care of The National Trust for Scotland and open to the public in the summer months.

From this position you can view the other side of the Lawnmarket, with buildings dating from the 16th to 18th centuries. Even the few later frontages are often a mere skin over much older structures. One of the buildings shows slightly overhanging upper storeys, one of the very few timber-framed buildings surviving in the old town.

South side of Lawnmarket

We shall explore some of these closes shortly, but first cross the street and bear right for a few yards until you reach a short narrow lane which is the head of the **West Bow**. Until the late 18th century, the West Bow was the only entrance to the city from the west, an ancient, steep and winding street ascending from the open space of the Grassmarket to the Lawnmarket. In the 1840s the West Bow, however picturesque it might have been, was condemned as unfit for modern living and a new street (Victoria Street, of course!) cut a swathe through the teeming closes, incorporating only the lower end of the old West Bow. The upper end, where you now are, stands as it did but has lost all its ancient houses, and the connection between the two ends of the West Bow is now a flight of steps.

Go down this short street, ignore the steps leading down to Victoria Street and turn right along a raised terrace until you have a view over the lower end of the West Bow which ends in the Grassmarket at the bottom of the hill, and pause here. If you look back the way you came, the present view has changed substantially from that of 150 years ago; then it would be a mass of tall houses and closes descending the steep hill to the Cowgate, which is not visible from where you stand but is the street at the bottom of the valley roughly parallel to the Royal Mile and which connects with the Grassmarket.

The lower end of the old West Bow is not completely lost. Below you on your right is an attractive row of 16th to 18th-Century houses with handsome gables of various heights and styles, which has been described as "one of the best groups of Old Street Architecture in Scotland," and which gives a good idea of how the street must once have looked.

At the bottom of the hill you will see one of the old well-heads, and here at the end of the Grassmarket stood the town gallows used up to the 18th century. It was the custom in Scotland for condemned criminals to walk to their execution, and an English army officer domiciled in Edinburgh in the 18th century admired this practice, which he considered more dignified than the English method of dragging the victim to the gallows in a

Roofscape
Lower West Bow

cart or a hurdle. This last walk, usually conducted in respectful silence, was from the Tolbooth prison near St Giles, up the Lawnmarket and down the West Bow, and the windows and doorways of these old houses were in great demand as a viewpoint on these occasions. This sad procession was commonplace in the "killing times" of the late 17th century as condemned Covenanters descended the West Bow to "glorify God in the Grassmarket", and Graham of Claverhouse (page 27) himself used one of these windows to observe the end of the Covenanters he had so ruthlessly hunted.

Later, in 1745 when the city was threatened by Prince Charles Edward's army, an attempt was made by the city fathers to rally the townspeople to its defence. As the reluctant assemblage was marched to the bottom of the West Bow, it shrank noticeably as small groups disappeared into the maze of alleyways leading from it, so that by the time it reached the Grassmarket only a handful remained! In the event it mattered little, since at the same time the Town Council was holding an emergency meeting about the situation in St Giles Cathedral, and the meeting while still in progress was presented with a courteous note from the Prince himself whose army had entered the city sooner than expected, requesting surrender of the city to which the Council was obliged to agree.

During the occupation which followed, the area of the West Bow over which you are now looking became something of a no-man's land between the Prince's army in the town and the remains of the Hanoverian army, which was penned up in the Castle but sent out patrols into this area. It is said that one of these patrols narrowly missed capturing the Prince himself, who was visiting the Lord Provost in his house in the West Bow, and that he only escaped by using a secret passageway leading to the Grassmarket.

Ahead of you, beyond the Grassmarket, you will see the turrets of George Heriot's School. Heriot was a wealthy 16th-

The towers of George Heriot's School seen over the roofline of the Grassmarket

Century businessman and philanthropist to whom King James VI was indebted for many a loan. He died in 1623 and endowed this school, and building began in 1628. Oliver Cromwell annexed it as a hospital for his wounded, but thereafter it reverted to its original purpose as a school, and has now served generations of Edinburgh boys for over 300 years.

Retrace your steps back to the Lawnmarket. To your left the top of the Royal Mile extends to the Castle Esplanade; it contains several features of interest which can be incorporated into a trip to the Castle, but is not part of this walk. Turn right without crossing and pass under the archway into **Riddle's Court** and **Riddle's Close**.

Facing you in Riddle's Court is the house in which David Hume the philosopher lived in 1751 and in which he wrote much of his *History of England*. Pass on further through another ancient archway ahead of you, and you enter a second courtyard which is a charming example of 16th-Century living, very peaceful and virtually unaltered through the centuries (see illustration, page 24). Numerous little doorways lead upwards, downwards and to cellars. The house facing you is of no great height within the courtyard, but because it is built on a steep slope like so many in the Royal Mile it is several storeys higher at the back, and a portion of its lower reaches can be seen at the back of shops in Victoria Street far below. Its simple exterior also belies an interior rich in fine panelled rooms with painted ceilings and great fireplaces.

This house belonged to Bailey Macmorran (see page 23) and it was through the door on the left that he emerged for the last time on 15th September 1595 on his way to quell the High School riot which resulted in his death. Here too was held the banquet for King James VI and his court in 1598.

As you return to the Lawnmarket note the bronzed plaque at the entrance to the close. You will see many of these on your walk and they are worth reading for the extra bits of information they supply. Look across again at the handsome facade of Gladstone's land, then continuing to your right take a quick look into Fisher's Close and then enter **Brodie's Close**. Go to the end of the short close, ignoring if you can the hideous modern building where the lower end of the close once was, then stroll back and absorb the atmosphere of this ancient backwater — an atmosphere particularly beloved of leaders of 'Evening Ghost Walks', for in this close lived the notorious Deacon Brodie. In the 1780s when the house just to the left of the archway was already very old the first-floor apartment was occupied by a prosperous and respected citizen, Dean of the Incorporated Trades and a prominent member of the Town Council, Deacon Brodie.

Edinburgh had for several years been troubled by a series of audacious burglaries, and in the dead of night you might observe a figure in shabby clothes and mask passing stealthily out through this archway, his pocket full of skeleton keys. It is a long and very dramatic story, but eventually Deacon Brodie was betrayed and fled abroad, then extradited and executed along with one of his accomplices on October 1st 1788. There was a record turnout round the scaffold outside St Giles, only a few steps away from here, for he had been a very charming and popular man with many friends, and the city was both scandalised and fascinated by his fate. His activities are certainly a mystery for he did not need the money — he probably just did it for the secret thrill of a double life and for the challenge to his skill, as he was a cabinet-maker by trade and a very clever engineer, and made his own skeleton

keys from wax impressions — these are now in the Museum
of Antiquities. The door to his apartment and its lock were
made by Brodie himself, and for the Town Council he had
previously fulfilled a special order, namely the design of the
new gallows, which he commented on wryly before being the
first to test it out himself!

On your left facing the arch to the Lawnmarket is a small
restaurant which provides a good cup of coffee or a simple snack,
and if you are ready for this go in and look around you, for this

The ancient vaulted kitchen of Deacon Brodie's House still serves
the same purpose in a modern café

was Deacon Brodie's workshop, where no doubt he worked on
his skeleton keys. At the end of the room is a fine vaulted
chamber which was the kitchen of his house.

Turn right out of Brodie's Close and cross at the traffic
lights, leaving the Lawnmarket for the next section of the
Royal Mile, the High Street. The road you have crossed is one
of the two built to connect the New Town with South
Edinburgh in the early 19th century, and although this
involved considerable destruction the axis of the Royal Mile
was not disturbed.

Facing us is St Giles Cathedral (see illustration, page 21), set in what is now an open space but was not always thus. Up to the beginning of the 19th century the Cathedral was hemmed in by ancient buildings, including the Tolbooth prison which features in Scott's *The Heart of Midlothian.* To the right of the Cathedral are the Law Courts, their classical facade hiding the 17th-Century Parliament Hall with its magnificent hammerbeam roof. The Cathedral and Parliament Hall are of great interest and, like the Castle and Holyrood Palace, should be visited, but are not part of this walk. The outer walls of the Cathedral were unfortunately refaced in about 1830, but the interior is medieval and from the outside the crowned tower still shows original stonework of about 1500.

This area, with its many shops and booths once crowded round the great church, was the social and administrative centre of the city, as well as the political centre of Scotland until the Act of Union of 1707. Just below the Cathedral you will find the **Market Cross** (of which now only parts are original), and here many historical events took place, such as the proclamation by Prince Charles Edward of his father as King James III and important State Executions including those of the Marquis of Montrose, the Marquis of Argyll and the Regent Morton.

But the Market Cross was also the spot at which commercial business was conducted in the open air. The Royal Exchange, now the **City Chambers**, recessed in its courtyard almost opposite, was built in 1753–61 in the flush of renewed business confidence following the collapse of the 1745 Rebellion. However as noted in 1766 by the writer Tobias Smollett …"All the people of business at Edinburgh, and even the genteel company, may be seen standing in crowds everyday from one to two in the afternoon at a place where formerly stood a market cross … here the people stand in the open from force of custom, rather than move a few yards to an Exchange that stands empty on one side." As a Stock Exchange it was therefore something of a failure, and the building was

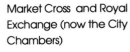

Market Cross and Royal Exchange (now the City Chambers)

Advocate's Close

later adapted as the City Council Chambers, which it still is. The first of the true "Georgian" buildings in the city, it has a certain ponderous elegance and is quite low in height on this side, but because of the slope of the ridge when viewed from Princes Street it is a massive building eleven storeys high. Obviously the 18th-Century building works involved destruction of several ancient closes, but rather curiously one of these (Mary King's Close) survives intact buried under the left-hand wing although at present inaccessible to the general public.

Go back a few steps, enter **Advocate's Close** and descend the short flight of stone stairs, taking in the view of Princes Street and the New Town ahead of you. Turn around the way you have come and note the fine turret staircase giving access at one time to the apartments of all classes of society as outlined on page 14. On your left are two fine doorways dated 1590, carved in relief with owners' initials and the usual pious texts — the original carved doors which I remember from the past have now been replaced with handsome but rather glossy modern doors.

The houses on the other side of the close have long been demolished, but in compensation we now have a view of a tall narrow house, once belonging to Bishop Adam Bothwell (page 22) who officiated at the Marriage of Mary Queen of Scots (page 20) to his namesake James Bothwell in 1567. The beautiful northern apse of this house (the end facing you) was completed early in the 17th century when the house belonged to Sir William Dick (page 26). Oliver Cromwell had his headquarters in the next close in 1650, and after the departure of Sir William is said to have enjoyed sitting in the top window of this apse viewing his navy in the Firth of Forth and gloating over the fall of his adversary.

Retrace your steps, leave Advocate's Close and continue down this side of the High Street. This portion of the street and many of the buildings would be instantly familiar to a citizen of the 17th or 18th century, and even later frontages often belie the ages of the buildings behind them. If you look down some of the closes, such as Anchor Close on the left or Borthwick's Close on the right, you will be aware of the steep descent from the crest of the ridge down which you are walking.

As you approach the second busy crossing, note the Tron Kirk on your right (see illustration, page 32). This is a 17th-Century building with a fine hammerbeam roof, but the whole church had to be reduced in size when the new road was cut through, and the steeple dates only from 1829 following a spectacular fire which destroyed the original steeple.

The Tron Kirk had a reputation for outspoken ministers, and one of these in 1693 prayed, "Lord have mercy on fools and idiots, and particularly on the Magistrates of Edinburgh."

The crossing you have now reached was the first of the two to be driven through the Old Town, and is known locally as 'The Bridges'. To your left is the North Bridge, the successor to the original bridge of 1772, the construction of which made the New Town possible. Beyond the bridge in the distance you will see the Register House, planned to complement the bridge and built in 1774 by Robert Adam with the proceeds of confiscated estates following the '45. To your right is the nineteen-arch South Bridge of 1785 spanning the Cowgate, from this point unrecognisable as a bridge due to the buildings lining it on each side. Beyond is the dome of The University, surmounting a handsome quadrangle dating from 1789(also by Robert Adam) and built on the site of much older University buildings.

Wherever it was planned that the road from the North Bridge was to cross the line of the High Street there was going to be a problem of levels. In fact the High Street was lowered at this crossing by several feet, but further desirable lowering was frustrated by the presence beneath the street of numerous ancient foundations and cellars, one of these latter being the 'Union Cellar' referred to on page 28, where the Act of Union was finally signed in 1707.

High Street from John Knox's House

After crossing at the lights and walking a few more yards pause for a moment and visualise the High Street before the busy intersection was made. It was unusually wide and lined with tall buildings, and Daniel Defoe in *A Tour of Great Britain* described it as "the largest, longest and finest street for Buildings and Number of Inhabitants, not in Britain only, but in the World." The Gentleman's Magazine of 1745 stated, "With regard to the High Street in general, it may be observed that its length and width, beauty and magnificence are, by travellers, said to be excelled by none in Europe, and it is really far from being equalled in London."

On your right across the street is the huge mass of the modern Scandic Crown Hotel, a well-intentioned but rather overpowering attempt to match the style of old Edinburgh. A large group of tall 17th-Century buildings, some of them seven floors high, was destroyed quite recently in the making of it, and the old nameplates of the lost closes are forlornly and rather guiltily displayed at their original sites on the hotel frontage.

When you reach Bailie Fyfe's Close on the left, stand in its entrance and look across the road to the top of Blackfriars Street, where you will see on the right an ancient house with a projecting staircase and fine carved entrance. This, now a young people's hostel, was the town house of The Regent Morton (see page 22), and through this doorway he left his home for the last time before trial and beheading by 'the maiden' in 1581. A 19th-Century drawing shows the front of the house with fine projecting timber galleries as described on page 16, a more interesting appearance than the present plain frontage and a reminder that many of the old stone fronts we now see were once adorned in this way.

This portion of the High Street becomes conspicuously narrowed by a house projecting into it from the left. This is **John Knox's House** (see page 19) and although his ownership is not conclusively proved, this long-held belief saved it from

Detail of John
Knox's House

demolition when the Victorians contemplated widening the High Street at this point. Certainly the house was already there in Knox's time, and was previously owned by Mary Queen of Scots' goldsmith James Mossman, whose initials J.M. are carved on the outside. It is a very curious and lovely house, a fine stone building showing all the features of a 16th-Century town dwelling — picturesque timber galleries and gables, pious mottoes, and an outside staircase. Inside are fine chambers, with richly painted ceilings full of primitive images. By means of careful restoration during this century the old house has slowly given up its secrets — in the 1930s some of the outside woodwork was stripped away revealing the inscriptions and statuary; in the 1960s painted panelling was fully exposed; and quite recently, behind the ground-floor panelling medieval shop-booths have come to light, indicating that this part at least may be even older than has been thought.

The ground floor is still a shop, and the upstairs rooms are open to the public and a delight to explore, with views back up the High Street which would have been quite familiar to John Knox or his contemporaries.

If on this visit you have no time to go into the house, just stand for a moment under the ancient overhanging beams at the corner of the house, and look back at the three churches of the Royal Mile. The adjacent house over the close is Moubray House, as old or possibly older than Knox's house. It has a fine outside stair and

Moubray House

a very narrow frontage, but is four times deeper behind. This will be apparent if you walk down Trunk Close, the narrow and atmospheric passageway between the two houses unchanged over five centuries.

Now cross the road and enter **Tweeddale Court**. Just inside the entrance there occurred in 1806 a celebrated incident known as The Begbie Tragedy, namely the horrific murder of a British Linen Bank messenger of that name, who was carrying a large sum of money from another branch and was found lying here with a large knife buried in him to the hilt. This was clearly a planned and premeditated crime since a sheet of paper was found fixed over the hilt of the weapon to prevent the murderer being covered with blood. Remarkably this was all carried out in broad daylight within sight and sound of the High Street crowds, yet there were no witnesses and the crime remained unsolved, although a package containing the larger-denomination notes was later found in the cavity of an old wall outside the city.

At the end of the court is the building that in Begbie's day housed the British Linen Bank. It dates from 1576 although the

Surviving section of City Wall in Tweeddale Court. There is a local belief that the lean-to shed against the wall was a sedan chair store

frontage which you see is largely a 17th-Century addition, and was originally the town house of the Marquess of Tweeddale.

Another feature of great interest is a substantial length of the medieval city wall surviving on the west side of the courtyard, exposed by the demolition of buildings with which it had become incorporated over the centuries. Its line when extended back to the High Street connected it to the Netherbow Port, the largest and most handsome gateway into the city. Prince Charles Edward and his army took this gateway by a ruse in 1745 and entered the city through it. Sadly this handsome structure was demolished fifteen years later, partly as a political gesture by the Prince's old Hanoverian enemies but also because the walls were no longer required and the gateway was becoming an obstruction to traffic.

Thus on leaving the courtyard (sparing a thought for poor Begbie), turning right past the site of the old Netherbow Port and crossing what was once an important junction, we have left the walled city and are entering the Canongate, which remained an independent burgh until 1856. After crossing the junction glance to your right down St Mary's Street, and in the distance you will catch a glimpse of a further substantial section of the city wall. Other stretches of the wall also survive, but lie outside the limits of this walk.

Stone-carved insignia of the Shoemakers' craft over the doorhead of Shoemakers Land in the Canongate

Although inevitably a great deal has been lost (even in my lifetime) and much restoration of the remainder has taken place, there are still many old houses of the 17th and 18th centuries to admire in the Canongate, all with history and tales too many to recount here.

Until the Court left Edinburgh for London in 1603, the Canongate by virtue of its proximity to Holyrood Palace and its more spacious ambience outside the confines of the city walls was essentially the residence of the courtiers and the nobility. On your right is one of the finest of their aristocratic mansions, **Moray House**, built in 1628 for Mary, Countess of Home. It is solidly constructed and fairly plain externally, but internally has large, lofty rooms with exquisitely beautiful moulded ceilings. The handsome gardens which once lay behind are now an open area thronged with students, since the term 'Moray House' has become synonymous with teacher-training in Scotland. A small stone summer-house in the grounds was the site of a historic event in 1707, namely the signing of The Act of Union of the Parliaments. To be accurate the signing took place at several sites due to the attentions of a

Moray House

hostile mob, as described on page 28. The summer-house still stands, now rather forlorn in a vehicle access road accessible from the Cowgate.

The pillars of the entrance gateway are surmounted by large stone spires, and between these pillars have passed many figures of history — King Charles I, Oliver Cromwell, King Charles II, and the Marquis of Argyll (see page 25) who owned the house in the early 17th century and who was the most powerful lord supporting the Covenant and thus allied to Oliver Cromwell and his cause. In 1648 Cromwell lodged here with the Marquis, and the two of them consulted on the "necessity to take away the King's life."

However the most dramatic event, only two years later, relates to the stone balcony which you see overhanging the street. On 16th May 1650, a few months after the execution of King Charles I, the wedding took place of the Marquis of Argyll's son, Lord Lorne, to the daughter of Lord Moray. The wedding party appeared on this balcony as Argyll's mortal enemy the Marquis of Montrose ('The Great Marquis', see page 25), finally betrayed and defeated, was borne up the Canongate, tied to a cart and surrounded by a mob whipped up into noisy hostility by the Covenanting ministers. The cart stopped beneath the balcony, and Montrose turned to face Argyll. Argyll flinched under his steady gaze, and the wedding party and the crowd below fell silent — all that is except Lady Jean Gordon, Argyll's niece, who continued to insult and jeer at Montrose, whereupon the crowd turned on her, shouting up "that it became her better to sit upon the cart for her adulteries." Argyll and his wedding guests crept back through the window and, according to W.E. Aytoun's famous poem, the mob "that came to scoff at him now turned aside and wept."

The Marquis of Montrose continued up the Canongate to trial at the Parliament Hall and was subsequently hanged at the Market Cross outside, bearing himself with dignity to the last … "he climbed the lofty ladder as it were the gate to heaven."

Today the scene outside Moray House has changed so little

that the historical imagination can easily evoke the atmosphere of that day in 1650 — the milling crowd, the controlled dignity of Montrose in his cart, the gaily dressed wedding party on the balcony, and the dramatic silence following Lady Gordon's crude outburst.

Next on the left you reach the **Canongate Tolbooth**, conspicuous with its bell tower and spire, outside stair, corbelled turrets, projecting clock and fine windows. It was built in 1592 as the civic centre and prison of the separate burgh of the Canongate but has served many functions over the centuries, and is now an enjoyable and fairly lighthearted Museum of Edinburgh Life.

Opposite is **Huntly House**, one of the very few surviving jettied and part-timberframed buildings, built in 1570 and remarkable for the number of carved texts on its frontage — it is now a City Museum. Pass under the archway into **Bakehouse Close**, a very attractive ancient courtyard flanked by Sir Archibald Acheson's house of 1633.

Huntly House

The Canongate Church, next to the Tolbooth, was built in 1688 for the congregation of the Abbey Church of Holyrood when they were turned out by the Catholic King James VII (James II of England). It is of Dutch style and not particularly suited to its location, but its graveyard contains some interesting tombstones, including that of Adam Smith, the 18th-Century political economist, whose devotees still come from many lands to visit his grave (just to the left of the gate).

The lowest stretch of the Canongate has been somewhat altered and modernised in recent years, but continue down and on the left enter the pend into **White Horse Close**. The attractive building at the end of the close, once an inn and the starting point of the stage-coach to London, has a dividing outside stair leading into two large overhanging timbered gables. The intervening dormer window bears the date of the building, 1623, and other smaller 17th-Century buildings flank the courtyard. In recent years the close has been tidied up

The White Horse Inn

and somewhat prettified, but it is still possible to picture the courtyard full of men and horses and the general confusion of an army at war, for this was the Officers' Headquarters of Prince Charles Edward's army in 1745.

We are nearing the end of our walk. Passing a rather fine 17th-Century building on the left overlooking the junction, cross the road into the Precincts of Holyrood Palace. Beyond this point a fugitive from justice could escape pursuit by claiming

Sanctuary of the Abbey, a right which lasted until 1881 when imprisonment for debt was abolished. On the left is the Abbey Strand, a small complex of attractive old buildings which in the 16th and 17th centuries housed courtiers and palace officials. Inside are some fine moulded ceilings and medieval painted rafters.

Continue past the remains of the gate-house and its little tower on the right, dating from 1502 but showing traces of much older arcading which once formed the side of a vaulted passageway. Although Holyrood Palace is not a part of this walk,

North-West Tower of Holyrood Palace. Queen Mary's apartments are on the second floor, and it was here on March 9th 1566 that David Rizzio was assassinated in the Queen's presence, the conspirators having gained access by the spiral staircase leading from Lord Darnley's apartments immediately below

from here you can admire its stately facade framed by the hills behind. Cromwell's troopers were billeted in the Palace during the Civil War and, famously careless of other people's property, accidentally started a fire which destroyed the South Wing. The towers on your left remain from the original building of 1505 and contain Mary Queen of Scots' apartments, where she was harangued by John Knox and where she witnessed the horrific murder of David Rizzio in 1566 (see page 20). The South Wing, seen on your right, contains handsome state apartments and the Picture Gallery where Prince Charles Edward held his glittering levee in 1745, this wing having been skilfully reconstructed in 1671 to match the original structure by King's Master Mason Robert Mylne, the same who devised Mylne's Court through which we first entered the Old Town.

Our walk ends here. Stroll back up the Royal Mile, or take any bus from the bus stop on your left back to The Bridges or the Lawnmarket. From there you can walk across the North Bridge or go down The Mound or through the closes back to Princes Street.

You have seen a great deal, although necessarily a selection. If you have enjoyed the historic atmosphere, explore more deeply into the closes and courtyards of Old Edinburgh on another visit, and you will be rewarded by unexpected pleasures every time.